D1527293

THIS NOTEBOOK BELONGS TO

....

Made in the USA
Las Vegas, NV
06 November 2022

58870439R00066